# Summer Solutions.

Minutes a Day-Mastery for a Lifetime!

# Level 5

# English Grammar & Writing Mechanics

Nancy McGraw and Nancy Tondy

Bright Ideas Press, LLC
Cleveland, OH

# Summer Solutions Level 5
# English Grammar & Writing Mechanics

All rights reserved. No part of this publication may be reproduced or transmitted in any form or by any means, electronic or mechanical, including photocopy, recording, or any information storage or retrieval system. Reproduction of these materials for an entire class, school, or district is prohibited.

**Printed in the United States of America**

ISBN: 978-1-934210-06-2

*Cover Design*: Dan Mazzola
*Editors*: Kimberly A. Dambrogio
Christopher Backs
*Illustrator*: Christopher Backs

Copyright © 2011 by Bright Ideas Press, LLC
Cleveland, Ohio

## Instructions for Parents/Guardians

- *Summer Solutions* is an extension of the *Simple Solutions* Approach being used by thousands of children in schools across the United States.

- The 30 lessons included in each workbook are meant to review and reinforce the skills learned in the grade level just completed.

- The program is designed to be used three days per week for ten weeks to ensure retention.

- Completing the book all at one time defeats the purpose of sustained practice over the summer break.

- Each book contains answers for each lesson.

- Each book also contains the Help Pages which list vocabulary, parts of speech, editing marks, and rules for capitalization, punctuation, and spelling.

- Lessons should be checked immediately for optimal feedback.

- Adjust the use of the book to fit vacations. More lessons may have to be completed during the weeks before or following a family vacation.

# Summer Solutions Level 5
## English Grammar & Writing Mechanics

## Reviewed Skills Include

- Punctuation and Capitalization
- All Parts of Speech
- Common Spelling Rules
- Proofreading and Revising with Editing Marks
- Sentence Structure / Parts of a Sentence
- Correcting Fragments and Run-ons
- Subject-Verb Agreement
- Vocabulary Building and Use of Resources
- Contractions and Abbreviations
- Cause and Effect
- Synonyms / Antonyms
- Homophones
- Fact and Opinion
- Use of Similes and Metaphors
- Analyzing Information in Charts and Graphs
- Writing Practice

**Help Pages begin on page 63.**

**Answers to Lessons begin on page 73.**

# Lesson #1

1. Find the meaning and pronunciation of the word *gaunt* in a dictionary. Place a ✓ next to any statement that is true.

   \_\_\_\_ *Gaunt* rhymes with *haunt*.

   \_\_\_\_ The word *gaunt* is a verb.

   \_\_\_\_ The opposite of *gaunt* is *plump*.

2. Add commas before and after the interrupting phrase.

   My mother wherever she is will expect a phone call from me.

3. Underline the correct verb form in this sentence.

   The puppies (is / were) living under the porch.

4. Write the words that make up the contraction.

   The daisies should've bloomed by now.          _____

5. Which of the following is an exclamation?

   A) We will be going camping this summer.
   B) Wait, maybe you can come with us!
   C) Why don't you ask your parents?
   D) Ask if you can bring your bike.

6. What does an exclamatory sentence do?

   A) tells something
   B) gives a command
   C) shows strong feeling
   D) An exclamatory sentence may do all of these.

For the next three sentences, choose *linking, helping,* or *action* to tell what kind of verb is underlined.

7. Those hamburgers <u>smell</u> great!

       linking      helping      action

8. Please set the table, and <u>pour</u> the drinks.

       linking      helping      action

9. We <u>will</u> eat as soon as the hot dogs are grilled.

       linking      helping      action

10. Is the underlined word an adjective or an adverb?

    Corrine swims <u>well</u>, but she needs to build endurance.

        adjective      adverb

**Proof It!** Rewrite the sentences correctly.

11. Krissy she is going to join "vacation bookworms."

    _____

    _____

12. It's a book club that meets at the (libary) all summer.

    _____

    _____

# Lesson #2

1. Find the word *evident* in a thesaurus or dictionary. Underline its meaning.

    mistaken    suspicious    clear    dangerous

2. Add commas.

    Michael our skateboard instructor won't let us on the ramps without elbow and knee pads.

3. Underline the correct verb in this sentence.

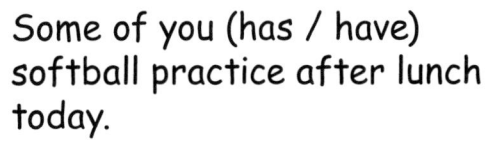

    Some of you (has / have) softball practice after lunch today.

4. Which contraction is spelled correctly?

    mighta've    could've    woulda'

5. Change these adjectives to adverbs by adding the suffix –*ly*. Write the adverbs below.

    short → _____

    wild → _____

    pleasant → _____

6. **Remember, adjectives modify nouns or pronouns. Adverbs modify verbs.** Underline the adjective; circle the adverb.

    The boys slept well in the new tent.

Summer Solutions© Grammar & Writing    Level 5

7. Join these two sentences with a conjunction. Write the compound sentence below.

    Richard is great at building things. He wants to be an architect.

    _____

    _____

8. Circle the simple subject.

    Larry, my cousin from Texas, always spends the Fourth of July with us.

**Proof It!** Read these sentences and then complete the last four items.

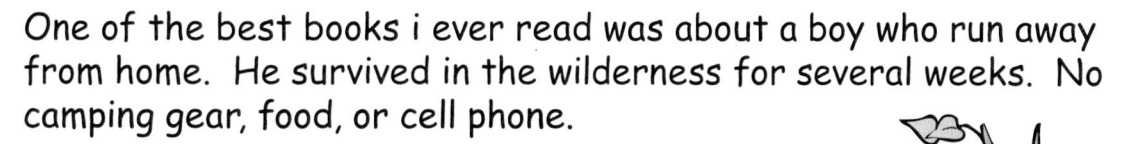

    One of the best books i ever read was about a boy who run away from home. He survived in the wilderness for several weeks. No camping gear, food, or cell phone.

9. Underline the sentence that has no errors.

10. Draw a line through the fragment.

11. Rewrite the fragment as a complete sentence.

    _____

    _____

12. Use two editing marks to correct other errors.

# Lesson #3

1. Find these words in a thesaurus or dictionary. Underline the word that best completes the sentence.

   amplify     diverge     protrude

   A handheld microphone will _____ your voice so that it can be heard throughout the auditorium.

2. Add commas before and after the interrupting phrase.

   Troy Smith the Heisman Trophy winner played football at The Ohio State University.

3. The relative pronoun in this sentence is underlined. Circle its antecedent.

   The university <u>that</u> he attended has an enrollment of over 50,000 students.

4. Write each contraction.     it is → _____

   she will → _____     they had → _____

5. What is the complete subject of this sentence? Draw a line under it.

   The House of Representatives has its schedule posted online.

6. Is the underlined word an *adjective* or an *adverb*?

   Tracy did a <u>good</u> job of cleaning out the garage.

   adjective     adverb

7. Choose the correct comparative.

   When she saw her report card, Sheila was (more upset / upsetter) than Mom was.

Summer Solutions© Grammar & Writing                                              Level 5

This bar graph shows the average daily attendance at Parkview Swimming Pool for the month of June. The pool opened on Saturday, June 9. Use the graph to answer the next five questions.

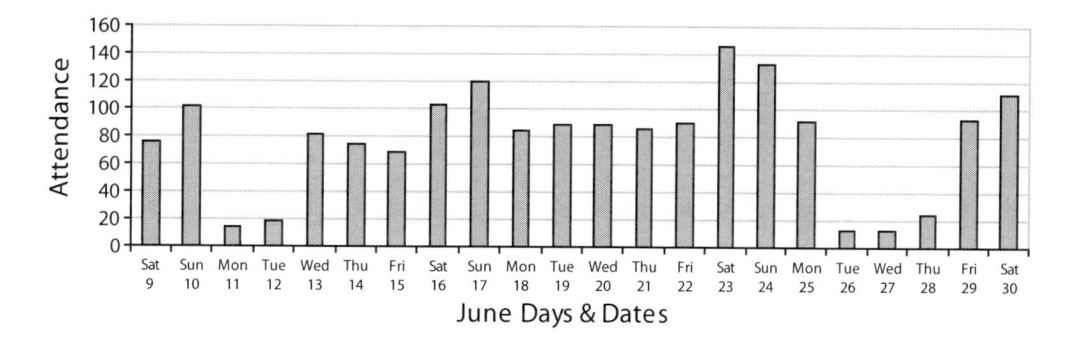

[Bar graph showing Attendance (y-axis, 0–160) vs. June Days & Dates (x-axis: Sat 9, Sun 10, Mon 11, Tue 12, Wed 13, Thu 14, Fri 15, Sat 16, Sun 17, Mon 18, Tue 19, Wed 20, Thu 21, Fri 22, Sat 23, Sun 24, Mon 25, Tue 26, Wed 27, Thu 28, Fri 29, Sat 30)]

8. What was the date of the first <u>weekday</u> that the pool was open?

   _____

9. By looking at the graph, can you tell which days may have been rainy or cold? List the dates here.

   _____

10. The lifeguards are assigned according to the number of people at the pool. If there are 50 people, there are three lifeguards; if there are 75 people, there are four lifeguards; if there are 100 people, there are five lifeguards, and so on. On which dates did the pool need five or more lifeguards?

    _____

11. According to the graph, which two days of the week seem to be the most popular for swimming?

    Sat.    Sun.    Mon.    Tues.    Wed.    Thurs.    Fri.

12. What necessary information is missing from this graph?

    A) the manager's name      C) the daily temperature
    B) a title                 D) the number of lifeguards

# Lesson #4

1. What is the meaning of the underlined word?

    Charlie is a comical guy, but his <u>shenanigans</u> get him into trouble.

        stories        buddies        mischief

2. Underline two interrogative pronouns.

    What is your phone number, and where do you live?

3. Cross out the contractions that are misspelled.

    shouldn't      shoulda'      would'nt      you'd

4. Draw a line under the complete predicate in this sentence.

    Shade-loving flowers grow nicely near the tree line.

5. **Adverbs describe verbs.** Underline the adverb; write the verb it modifies.

    Read the question carefully, and write your answer. _____

6. You can find a list of irregular comparatives in the *Help Pages*. Select the correct comparative.

    I wasn't feeling well this morning, but now I am (gooder / better / best).

7. What is the purpose of a bibliography?

    A) to give credit to authors

    B) to allow the reader to check the information in a report

    C) to list sources

    D) all of these

Summer Solutions© Grammar & Writing — Level 5

8. Underline the interjection.

    Oh no! The radiator is overheating.

9. Which of these is an example of a simile?

    A) Theresa is a lifesaver.
    B) Having Theresa around is like having an extra set of hands.
    C) I have a million things to do today!

10. What two things are being compared in the simile above?

    _____

11. Does the sentence below have a direct object? If you answered "yes," what is the direct object?

    _____ Yes     _____ No

    Louise and Joy built a tree house in the back yard.

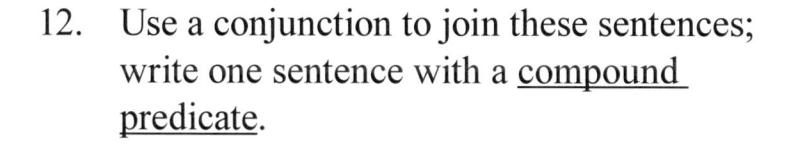

    _____

12. Use a conjunction to join these sentences; write one sentence with a compound predicate.

    A tree house is a great place to read a book. A tree house is a great place to take a nap.

    _____

    _____

# Lesson #5

1. Complete the analogy.

    funny : funnier :: cold : _____

    coldest      colder      hot

2. Add two commas to this sentence.

    We made cinnamon rolls my mother's favorite to serve with the soup.

3. Choose the adjective that makes sense.

    If you scratch your skin the rash will get (worser / more / worse).

4. Replace the underlined word or words with a plural subject pronoun.

    <u>The giant pandas</u> are coming to the zoo this summer.  _____

5. Write a contraction to replace the underlined words.

    <u>I have</u> never seen a giant panda before, except on television.

    _____

6. What word does the underlined adverb modify?

A panda named Tai Shan <u>finally</u> arrived today. _____

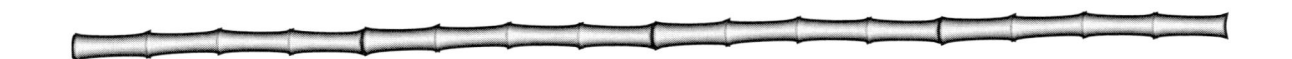

Read the paragraph, and look at the underlined parts. If there is a punctuation, capitalization, or spelling error choose the correction. If there is no error, choose "correct as is."

Biologists classify all living things into many categories that go from narrow to broad. <u>For example</u> the giant panda is unique because it is the
7.
only member of its <u>genus, "Ailuropoda."</u> The next classification after genus
8.
is <u>family and</u> the giant panda is a member of the bear <u>family the</u> panda is
9.                                                                              10.
also a carnivore (order), a mammal (class), a chordate (phylum), and of course,
<u>an animal</u> (kingdom). There are seven classifications <u>al together?</u>
11.                                                                              12.

Source: Giant Pandas at the Smithsonian National Zoo. http://nationalzoo.si.edu/Animals/Giant-Pandas/PandasForKids/classification/classification.htm 2006.

7. A) For example,
   B) For example;
   C) correct as is

8. A) genus "Ailuropoda".
   B) genus – 'ailuropoda.'
   C) correct as is

9. A) family, and
   B) family; and
   C) correct as is

10. A) families, the
    B) family. The
    C) correct as is

11. A) an Animal
    B) an animal.
    C) correct as is

12. A) altogether.
    B) all together?
    C) correct as is

# Lesson #6

For the first four items, write *C* if the underlined part states a *cause*; write *E* if the underlined part states an *effect*.

1. _____ Many beautiful lakes were formed <u>as the result of moving and melting glaciers</u>.

2. _____ <u>Weathering — the effect of wind and water</u> — causes rocks to break down and become soil.

3. _____ <u>Glaciers begin to melt</u> when the temperature rises.

4. _____ <u>The melting of glaciers</u> may lead to higher water levels in the oceans.

5. What is plagiarism?

    A) copying someone else's work
    B) citing your sources
    C) a bibliography
    D) none of these

6. Underline each word pair that could make a contraction.

    they had     he will     them have     she have

7. Find the meaning and pronunciation of the word *archaic* in a dictionary. Place a ✓ next to any statement that is true.

   _____ The *h* in *archaic* is silent.

   _____ *Archaic* means "out-of-date."

   _____ An *archaic* is part of a building.

8. What does an interrogative sentence do?

   A) tells something   C) gives a command
   B) asks something   D) shows strong feeling

9. Underline the adverb in this sentence. What word does the adverb modify?

   If you wait patiently, you will get a turn.

   _____

10. Choose the adjective form that is correct.

    That is the (bestest / most good / best) movie I've seen all summer.

11. **Proof It!** Read the sentences below. Draw a line through the fragment.

    If I could meet a famous person, I would like it to be a United States President. The leader of the free world.

12. What could be added to the fragment that would make it a complete sentence?

    a subject     a prepositional phrase     a predicate     a pronoun

# Lesson #7

1. **Use commas before and/or after contrasting phrases that use *not*.** Add two commas to this sentence.

    We need to buy fruit not vegetables at the supermarket.

2. Which two words are synonyms?

    friend     companion     stranger     traveler

3. Underline the relative pronoun. Write its antecedent on the line.

    Dial the phone number that is on the back cover of the book.

    _____

4. Write these contractions.

    we had ➔ _____

    you would ➔ _____

    they would ➔ _____

5. Which of these is an example of a <u>metaphor</u>?

    A) Theresa is a lifesaver.

    B) Having Theresa around is like having an extra set of hands.

    C) I have a million things to do today!

6. What two things are being compared in the metaphor above?

    _____     _____

Summer Solutions© Grammar & Writing                     Level 5

7. What does a declarative sentence do?

   A) tells something       C) asks something
   B) gives a command       D) shows strong feeling

Look at the underlined words. Decide whether each word is used as a *noun*, an *adjective*, or a *verb*. Then write the words in the proper categories.

All <u>winter</u> we <u>read</u> <u>funny</u> stories, and we <u>hike</u> along the <u>snowy</u> <u>trails</u> behind my grandmother's <u>house</u>.

8. Nouns      _____

   _____

9. Adjectives _____

   _____

10. Verbs     _____

    _____

11. Proofread the sentence below for spelling. Use the editing mark for "check spelling" to mark any errors.

    Some noticable improvments were made in the cafeteria.

12. Now that you have proofread the sentence, rewrite it correctly.

    _____

    _____

15

## Lesson #8

1. Insert commas before and after the contrasting phrase.

    Maureen not Aunt Chloe will be joining us.

2. Find these words in a thesaurus or dictionary. Underline the word that best completes the sentence.

    droll    solemn    triumphant

    The diplomat's funeral was a _____ ceremony.

3. List the two past tense forms of the verb *understand*.

    _____  has, have, or had _____

4. Draw a line between the subject and predicate in this sentence.

    Our spring concert featured vocal solos and several dance routines.

5. Which is an *adjective* and which is an *adverb*?  foolishly  funny

    _____                _____
    adjective                                              adverb

Look at the list of nouns; decide how each noun fits into the chart below. Write each noun where it belongs. The first one has been done for you.

Asia's    dreams    ~~Mt. Hood~~    bicycle    chipmunks'

| | Noun | Common | Proper | Abstract | Possessive | Singular | Plural |
|---|---|---|---|---|---|---|---|
| | Mt. Hood | | ✓ | | | ✓ | |
| 6. | | ✓ | | ✓ | | | ✓ |
| 7. | | ✓ | | | | ✓ | |
| 8. | | ✓ | | | ✓ | | ✓ |
| 9. | | | ✓ | | ✓ | ✓ | |

10. Add the suffix -*est* and write the new words on the line below.

    easy → _____    crazy → _____

11. Match these suffixes with their meanings.    -*phobia*    -*phone*    -*gram*

    _____ - sound    _____ - writing    _____ - fear

12. Rewrite the sentence correctly.

    Luna ~~she~~ is going to get braces as soon as (scool) starts.

    _____

    _____

# Lesson #9

1. Which underlined word is used as an *adverb*? Which is a *preposition*? (Remember, an adverb modifies another word; a preposition begins a prepositional phrase.) Write *A* or *P*.

    A) _____ Let's play <u>outside</u>.

    B) _____ The ball was knocked <u>outside</u> the foul line.

2. Identify the statement as either *fact* or *opinion*.

    Braces are used to correct teeth that are not aligned properly.

        fact          opinion

3. Insert a comma and a conjunction between the independent clauses.

    Many people have imperfect teeth _____ they do not need braces.

4. Use the editing mark for capitalization to correct two errors in the sentence.

    I see my orthodontist, dr. Sarhas, on saturdays.

5. Circle the subject of the sentence.

    Braces can be painful, since their job is to move teeth by applying pressure.

6. Write these postal abbreviations next to their names.

        PR         DE         AL

    ____Delaware     ____Puerto Rico     ____Alabama

7. Is *perfect* used as an *adjective* or a *verb* in the following sentence?

    The only way to perfect your skills is to practice them.

        adjective          verb

Read Sister Marie Celeste's recipe for Energy Fudge; then answer the next five questions. *Do not use this recipe if you are allergic to peanuts.

---

Energy Fudge*

| 2 C sugar | 1 C chunky peanut butter | 5 T cocoa |
| ½ tsp. salt | 1 tsp. vanilla | ½ C skim milk |
| ½ C butter | 3 C oatmeal | |

Ask an adult to help you, since you will be using the stove. You will need a 9 x 13 inch baking pan. Butter the pan, or spray it with non-stick cooking spray. Put the sugar, salt, butter, cocoa, and milk in a sauce pan. Heat it – while stirring – until it boils. Keep stirring, and boil the mixture for one full minute. Then remove the pan from the heat; add the peanut butter, vanilla, and oatmeal. Blend completely and spread the mixture in the baking pan. Cool fudge completely before cutting into squares.

---

8. Why is adult supervision recommended?

    A) to help with measuring    C) ingredients have to be cooked
    B) to read the directions    D) kids may have allergies

9. How many ingredients are needed to make Energy Fudge? _____

10. What must you do while heating the first five ingredients?

    _____

11. What should you do before you cut the fudge and serve it?

    _____

12. You should not try to make this fudge if _____.

    A) you do not have all of the ingredients.    D) any of these
    B) you are not allowed to use the stove.
    C) you are allergic to peanuts.

# Lesson #10

1. Complete the analogy.

    China : Asia :: Italy : _____

    Africa     Australia     Europe

2. Write the meanings of these contractions.

    haven't → _____        didn't → _____

3. What are the four types of sentences?

    _____        _____

    _____        _____

4. Underline the prepositional phrase, and circle the object of the preposition.

    We traveled throughout the Midwest.

5. Write **adjective** or **adverb** next to each sentence to name the part of speech that is underlined.

    A) _____ Kim will be <u>happy</u> to give you a ride to the park.

    B) _____ She can <u>easily</u> drop you off on her way to work.

6. What is plagiarism?

    A) copying someone's work     C) breaking copyright laws

    B) stealing another person's words     D) all of these

**Summer Solutions© Grammar & Writing**  Level 5

7. List the three articles. (Use the *Help Pages* if you're not sure what articles are.)

   _____   _____   _____

8. Rewrite each noun in its possessive form. The first one has been done for you.

   handlebars on the bicycle - the bicycle's handlebars

   roots of the tree - _____

   toys of the puppy - _____

9. Write the two past tense forms of the verb *get*.

   _____, has, have, or had _____

10. Match these word parts with their meanings.

    *-port*     not
    *geo-*      carry
    *non-*      earth

11. Choose the word with the most appropriate connotation for this sentence.

    The magician showed us some great (tricks / frauds).

12. **Proof It!** Rewrite the sentence with corrections.

    Peggi really enjoyed playing golf and hanging with her friends
                                               ∧
                                              out

    _____

    _____

# Lesson #11

1. Does the underlined part state a *cause* or an *effect*?

    Now that the grocery store in Mayville has closed, <u>shoppers have to travel to the next city to get food and supplies</u>.

            cause               effect

2. Add two commas to set off an interrupting phrase in this sentence.

    Use cloth napkins not paper for the luncheon.

3. Underline the relative pronoun in the sentence below. What is its antecedent?

    The key that we found at the skateboard park belonged to Michael.

    _____

4. Write the contraction for each of these.

    will not → _____     does not → _____

5. Draw a line under the complete subject of this sentence.

    The senators from Ohio met to discuss the school funding issues.

6. What is the subject of this sentence?

    Take your cell phone with you when you walk the dog.

    _____

Write the abbreviations for each of the following words

7. gallon _____

   yard _____

8. teaspoon _____

   ounce _____

9. dozen _____

   tablespoon _____

10. Choose the correct verb form.

    An earthquake has (shaked / shook / shaken) the floorboards loose.

11. Is the demonstrative in the sentence used as a *pronoun* or an *adjective*?

    My lunch is in the refrigerator, so <u>this</u> must be yours.

          pronoun          adjective

12. Write the plural form of each noun.

    wolf - _____    roof - _____

# Lesson #12

1. Use what you know about word parts to match each word with its meaning.

   _____ postpone          _____ polymorphic          _____ phobic

   A) fearful      B) put off until later      C) many forms

2. Underline an interrogative pronoun.

   Whom would you like to invite to your birthday party?

3. Write the meanings of these contractions.

   weren't ➔ _____      wasn't ➔ _____

4. What does an imperative do?

   A) tells something      C) asks something
   B) gives a command     D) shows strong feeling

5. Adverbs tell *how*, *when*, *where*, or to *what extent*. What does the adverb in this sentence tell?

   The Southland neighbors are having a yard sale <u>tomorrow</u>.

   when      how      where      to what extent

6. Correct a mistake in this sentence with an editing mark.

   This afternoon Mom will teach us how to make irish soda bread.

7. Choose the conjunction that best completes this sentence.

> The storm caused a power outage, (but / so / and / or) that won't spoil our fun.

8. In which list are all the plurals spelled correctly?

    A) taxs, crunches, lash's, boss
    B) taxes, crunches, lashes, bosses
    C) taxes, crunches, lashes, boss'
    D) taxes, crunches, lashez, bossez

9. Add a comma between the contrasting phrases.

> Hang your bathing suit on the clothesline not on the towel rack.

10. Choose the verb that agrees with the indefinite pronoun.

> (Have / Has) everybody gotten a drink of water?

11. Write the contraction for each of these.

    is not → _____

    are not → _____

12. Underline the action verb and circle the direct object in the sentence below.

> Day camp was fun today; we played a game called "Left, Right, Center."

# Lesson #13

1. Use context clues to determine the meaning of the underlined word.

    The cassette tapes that were popular in the twentieth century are <u>obsolete</u> now that we have CD's and MP3's.

        modern   confusing   desirable   outdated

2. Add commas.

    Use sugar not artificial sweetener in the lemonade.

3. Which is correct?

    A) Them are mine.    C) They are mine.
    B) Those are mines.   D) All of these are correct.

4. Complete the analogy.

    giant : enormous :: ancient : _____

        new      old      history

5. Is this a sentence?   All of the countries on the continent of Asia.

        Yes   No

6. Sort these words into two categories: *adjectives* and *adverbs*.

    lazy   merrily   hopeful   perfect   nicely   shortly

    Adjectives _____

    Adverbs _____

7. Add a comma and quotation marks.

    I never get a chance to be the leader chirped Betsy.

Summer Solutions© Grammar & Writing  Level 5

8. Remember, *good* is an adjective, so it modifies a noun; *well* is an adverb, so it may modify a verb. Write **good** or **well** to complete each sentence.

   Vince cleaned his room really _____. He even

   did a _____ job of washing the windows.

9. Which pair of correlative conjunctions will best complete the sentence?

   either / or     neither / nor     both / and

   You need to earn some money this summer; you can _____

   do yard work _____ baby-sit.

10. Use the editing mark for "check spelling" to mark any misspelled words.

    Hanson showed that he was gratful by tidying up the house.

11 – 12. Give your feedback. Read the paragraph, and complete the checklist below.

   I wish that I could get a robot that would do three things every day: clean my room, check my homework, and pack my lunch. I like to have a tidy room, but sometimes I don't feel like making my bed. When I am in a hurry, I just throw things on the floor, and before you know it, my room is a mess! Also, I do my homework every day, but I'm not always sure I did it correctly. Sometimes I forget to put my papers in my book bag. A homework robot could help with these things. Finally, I would like the robot to pack me a lovely lunch every day. Each day I would have something different and delicious like pizza, cheesy crackers, fruit salad, and peanut butter cookies.

   _____ Underline the topic sentence.

   _____ Circle some descriptive words or a phrase that you think is well-written.

# Lesson #14

1. Choose the pronoun that agrees with the subject.

    Several of the participants have already paid (his / their) entrance fees.

2. Write a contraction to replace the underlined words.

    The two-liter bottles <u>have not</u> been opened yet. _____

3. What is the simple subject of this sentence?

    Good nutrition leads to proper growth and a strong immune system.

4. An adjective often becomes an adverb by adding *-ly*. Use the adjective *light* and the adverb formed from *light* to complete the sentence.

    The rain fell _____ all evening, and

    there was a_____ mist in the morning.

5. **A concept is something you know about, but you can't see it or touch it.** Concepts are abstract nouns. Draw a line under each abstract noun.

    furniture    joy    memories    tractor    pride    calculator    generosity

6. Rewrite the sentence, using a possessive noun in place of the underlined phrase.

    The siren <u>of the police car</u> scared the bully away.

    _____

    _____

Summer Solutions© Grammar & Writing — Level 5

7. Choose the best word to show a cause-effect relationship.

   No one was ready to order, (since / so / because) the waiter walked away.

8. Underline any words that are <u>antonyms</u> of the word *ignorance*.

   knowledge   proficiency   unawareness   expertise   inefficiency

9. Write three coordinate conjunctions.

   _____     _____     _____

The label shows nutritional information for a type of cereal. Study the label and use it to answer the next three questions.

10. How many calories are in one serving of the cereal?

    _____

11. Does a serving of cereal have more carbohydrates or more protein?

    carbohydrates          protein

12. What percentage of the daily recommendation of dietary fiber is available in one serving?

    A) 3g
    B) 12%
    C) 114g
    D) 80%

**Nutrition Facts**

Serving Size ½ cup (114g)
Serving Per Container 4

**Amount Per Serving**

| Calories 90   Calories from Fat 30 | |
|---|---|
| | % Daily Value |
| **Total Fat** 3g | 5% |
| Saturated Fat 0g | 0% |
| **Total Cholesterol** 0mg | 0% |
| **Sodium** 300mg | 13% |
| **Carbohydrates** 13g | 4% |
| Dietary Fiber 3g | 12% |
| Sugars 3g | |
| **Protein** 3g | |

# Lesson #15

1 – 2. Write these nouns in their proper places in the chart below.

nation    Indians    people    Navaho

|  | Singular | Plural |
|---|---|---|
| Common | A) _____ | C) _____ |
| Proper | B _____ | D) _____ |

3. Underline two things that are compared in the following simile.

   Early that morning the sun appeared like a ripe yellow grapefruit in the sky.

4. Are the underlined words *synonyms* or *antonyms*?

   Patricia is a <u>skilled</u> journalist; she is <u>proficient</u> at all types of writing.

   synonyms    antonyms

5. Put a ✓ next to each sentence that tells what you should do in order to avoid plagiarism.

   A) _____ Properly cite your sources.

   B) _____ Download information from the internet.

   C) _____ Put quotation marks around a person's exact words.

   D) _____ Copy somebody else's writing.

6. Insert a comma, quotation marks, and an end mark.

   The scarecrow asked  Have you seen the Wizard

7. Underline the action verb; draw a ring around the direct object.

   Every three years we paint our deck.

8 – 12. Use this graphic organizer to write a short report about koalas. Write at least five complete sentences.

| Question | Answer | Details |
|---|---|---|
| What is a koala? | a marsupial; related to kangaroos, not bears | small, furry mammal (about 20 lbs. in weight) |
| Where do koalas live? | eastern Australia | in trees, bush land, and near other koalas |
| What do koalas eat? | leaves, mostly eucalyptus | there are hundreds of types of eucalyptus; koalas eat only a few types |
| Is the koala endangered? | yes, due to predators, disease, and loss of habitat | loss of habitat caused by land clearing, drought, bush fires |

# Lesson #16

Take a look at the table of Latin roots. Then match one of the examples with each of the meanings below.

| Root | Meaning | Examples |
|------|---------|----------|
| *trans* | across | transplant, transistor |
| *terr* | land | territory, terra cotta |
| *ped* | foot | pedal, pedestrian |

1. someone who travels by foot _____

2. to move a plant from one place to another _____

3. "baked earth" _____

4. Choose the correct word to complete the sentence.

    The basketball players sing (they're / there / their) chant before every game.

5. Underline the complete subject of this sentence.

    The Mothers Against Drunk Driving will have a rally in Public Square.

6. Choose the correct homophones.

    I asked the clerk (for / four) some paper, and she gave me (for / four) boxes.

7. Underline the adverb; write the verb it modifies.

   Aunt Betsy tenderly lifted the sleeping child. _____

Lisa's family tree shows Lisa, her parents, her grandparents, and her great-grandparents on both sides. Study Lisa's family tree and use it to answer the next five questions.

## Lisa Baer Family Tree

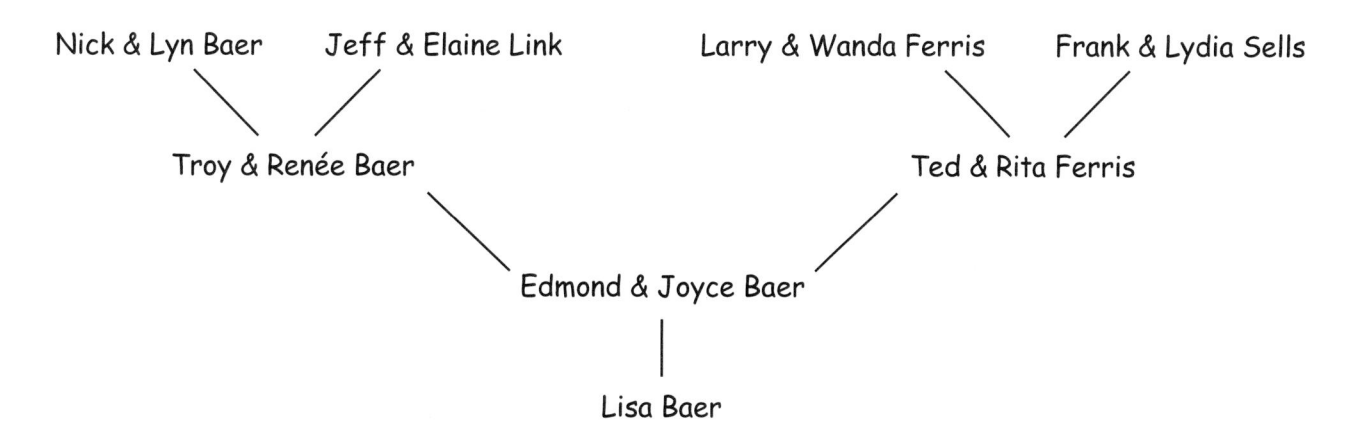

Nick & Lyn Baer    Jeff & Elaine Link        Larry & Wanda Ferris    Frank & Lydia Sells

   Troy & Renée Baer                              Ted & Rita Ferris

           Edmond & Joyce Baer

                Lisa Baer

8. Who are Lisa's parents?

   Frank & Rita    Joyce & Edmond    Ted & Rita    Troy & Renée

9. What are the first and last names of Lisa's grandmothers?

   _____

10. Which of these is Lisa's great-grandfather on her mother's side?

    Jeff Link    Troy Baer    Larry Ferris    Ted Ferris

11. Who are the parents of Renée Baer? _____

12. Whom did Ted Ferris marry? _____

## Lesson #17

1. Add a comma, quotation marks, and an end mark.

    Lexie answered I got my nickname from my little brother

2. Are the underlined words *synonyms* or *antonyms*?

    Rebuilding the <u>inferior</u> housing structure was an <u>ideal</u> project for the apprentices.

          synonyms        antonyms

3. In which list are all the plurals spelled correctly?

    A) chicken's, glases, pens, children
    B) chickenes, glasses, pens, children
    C) chickens, glasses, pens, children
    D) chickens, glass, pens, childs

Sort the pronouns and write each one in the proper list.

    many   who   your   everyone   their   that   my   which   someone

4. Indefinite _____

5. Relative _____

6. Possessive _____

7. Cross out the fragment.

    What is a person's most basic need?  Shelter, water, food, or safety?  These are all important for survival.

Summer Solutions© Grammar & Writing — Level 5

8. **Adverbs modify verbs.** Draw a line under the adverb in this sentence; write the verb it modifies.

    Lindy thoroughly examined the contents of the package.

    _____

9. Choose the correct articles.

    Who has tasted (a / an) pomegranate or (a / an) apricot?

10. Which is a *cause* and which is an *effect*? Write **C** or **E**.

    A) _____ Christopher Columbus thought he sailed to India;

    B) _____ that is why he called the people he met "Indians."

**Proof It!** Rewrite these two sentences correctly.

11. Columbus h̶e̶ ⁀was born in Italy, s̶i̶n̶c̶e̶ he sailed from Spain.
                                    but

    _____

    _____

12. There were three ships: the n̲ina, the p̲inta, and the s̲anta Maria.

    _____

    _____

# Lesson #18

1. Complete the analogy.

   cheese : dairy :: wheat : _____

   bread     rye     grain

2. Choose the word with the best connotation for this sentence.

   Don't use this extension cord; it may be (unsafe / perilous).

3. Replace the underlined word or words with a subject pronoun.

   <u>He and the boys</u> will join us at the campsite. _____

4. Join these two sentences with a conjunction. Write the compound sentence below.

   Florida is a peninsula. Its name means "full of flowers."

   _____

   _____

5. Add an apostrophe, two commas, and an end mark.

   Marks brother his father and his grandfather are all firefighters

6. Choose the correct article.

   This is (an / the / a) last unopened gallon of water.

7. In which of the sentences is the word *nice* used correctly?

   A) We had a very *nice* dinner with our neighbors.
   B) My little brother is learning to play *nice* with other kids.
   C) Both are correct.

8. When you use a book to get information for a report, what are you required to tell about the book? Check all that are true.

   _____ the author's name

   _____ name of the library or book store where you got the book

   _____ the title of book

   _____ the number of pages in the book

9. Remember, a **cause** tells *why*; an **effect** tells *what*. Read these sentences. Which is a *cause* and which is an *effect*?

   A) _____ Volunteer soldiers in Tennessee showed tremendous courage during the War of 1812.

   B) _____ For this reason, Tennessee is nicknamed "The Volunteer State."

10 – 12. Imagine that you could have a custom-built robot that would do three things for you every day. What three things would your robot do? Write your robot description below.

_____

_____

_____

_____

_____

_____

# Lesson #19

1. Add the proper punctuation to this sentence.

    Julia s tortilla soup was made with carrots onions peppers and beans

2. Rewrite this sentence correctly.

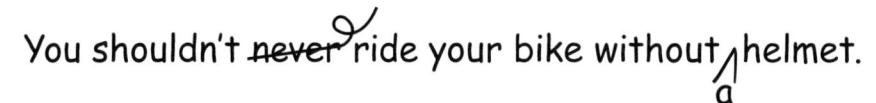

    You shouldn't ~~never~~ ride your bike without a helmet.

    _____

    _____

3. Underline an interrogative pronoun.

    Who is it you wanted to see?

4. Underline two things that are compared in the following simile.

    The fresh asparagus, banded together like a bundle of fresh new pencils, was placed in a pot of boiling water.

5. Are these words spelled correctly? Cross out any misspellings and write the correct forms below.

    collecttable    slightly    hankercheif

    _____

    _____

6. Insert the past tense form of the verb *mistake*. (If you're not sure, check the *Help Pages*.)

    I think someone may have _____ my suitcase for his.

7. Which is which? Write **adjective** or **adverb** above each underlined word.

The room is <u>pleasantly</u> decorated, and the flowers give off a <u>lovely</u> fragrance.

8. Is each statement a **fact** or an **opinion**?

   A) _____ The Dead Sea has a higher salt content than any other body of water on the earth.

   B) _____ Nothing can live in the Dead Sea, so its name is very appropriate.

Use the organizer to sort the following nouns into four categories.

flash drives   Spain   helmet   Pete   Mr. Muller   ivy
imagination   Honolulu   loyalty   Dr. Lilly   Pittsburgh   love

| 9. Persons | 10. Places | 11. Concrete Things | 12. Concepts or Abstract Nouns |
|---|---|---|---|
|  |  |  |  |

# Lesson #20

1 – 5. Complete the chart with words that begin with the letters at the left. A few examples have been done for you.

|   | Places | Foods | Animals | Vegetation |
|---|---|---|---|---|
| E | Edmonton |  |  |  |
| A |  | apple pie |  |  |
| R | Rwanda |  |  |  |
| T |  |  |  | tree fern |
| H |  |  |  | hyacinth |

6. Choose an antonym for the underlined word.

> The multi-colored panels covering the store-front created a <u>beautiful</u> effect.
>
> > hideous
> >
> > interesting
> >
> > familiar
> >
> > startling

7. Fill in the verb.

> Harriet was not messy, nor_____ she abrupt.

8. Fill in the plural possessive form of the word *child*.

> Please put the _____ coats and hats in the closet.

9. Choose the verb that agrees with the singular indefinite pronoun.

   Neither of the sisters (was / were) old enough to baby sit.

10. Is the underlined part a *cause* or an *effect*?

    The Portuguese ruled Brazil for many years, so <u>Portuguese is the official language of Brazil</u>.

            cause         effect

11. Write linking, action, or helping to identify each underlined verb.

    The clown <u>is</u> funny, and he <u>can</u> <u>make</u> balloon animals for all the kids.
            A                 B   C

    A) _____

    B) _____

    C) _____

12. **Proof It!**

    The most newest state in the United States is hawaii.

    Is this sentence correct?     Yes     No

    If the sentence is not correct, rewrite it correctly.

    _____

    _____

# Lesson #21

1. Add an apostrophe, commas, quotation marks, and an end mark.

   Lets walk to the skateboard park suggested Erica and we can get an ice cream cone on the way

2. Which is correct?

   A) Their here!
   B) Your late
   C) We're hungry!
   D) All of these are correct.

3. Write a contraction to replace the underlined words.

   It will be fine. _____

4. Complete the sentence with **good** or **well**.

   Charlotte is an excellent programmer, and she speaks _____ also.

5. Underline the adjective; write the noun it describes.

   The scouts quickly set up the tent and organized a tidy campsite.

   _____

6. Is it okay to print information from the Internet and include it in a report for school? Explain your answer.

   _____

   _____

   _____

Summer Solutions© Grammar & Writing                                Level 5

7. What is the <u>connotation</u> of the underlined phrase in this sentence?

   I don't think Dave will buy a video game; he is <u>miserly</u> with his allowance.

   A) thrifty     B) tight-fisted     C) generous     D) insensible

8. Write out this date; use correct capitalization and punctuation.

   12-21-06 _____

9. Underline the verb phrase.

   The Wilsons are hosting a holiday party.

   What is the main verb? _____   What is the helping verb? _____

10. Underline the relative pronoun in this sentence. Circle its antecedent.

    I took the jacket that I found to the information desk.

11. Which group of words is a fragment?

    A) For my birthday we all went roller skating.
    B) Then we ate pizza and played some video games.
    C) It was a blast! Next year I want to have a swim party.
    D) Or maybe paintball and lunch at McDonald's.

12. **Proof It!**

    Me and Josie share the same birthday.

    Is this sentence correct?                      Yes        No
    If the sentence is not correct, rewrite it correctly.

    _____

43

# Lesson #22

1. Which underlined word is used as an **adverb**? Which is a **preposition**?

    A) Take a few minutes to look <u>around</u>.  _____

    B) Put a rubber band <u>around</u> the stack of cards.  _____

Choose *linking*, *helping*, or *action* to tell what kind of verb is underlined in each sentence.

2. The Sears Tower in Chicago <u>is</u> one of the world's tallest buildings.

    linking     helping     action

3. Sears, Roebuck & Company <u>built</u> the Tower in the early 1970's.

    linking     helping     action

4. The Empire State Building <u>had</u> been built in the 1930's.

    linking     helping     action

5. Underline the complete subject of this sentence.

    The Bank of China in Hong Kong is over seventy stories high.

6. Choose an adverb to complete this sentence.

    The defense lawyers knew that the judge had always ruled (just / justly).

7. Underline the adjective. Circle the noun it describes.

   The Chrysler Building in New York is gigantic.

8. Rewrite the sentence. Use a possessive noun in place of the underlined phrase.

   The tallest building <u>of the world</u> is in Taiwan.

   _____

   _____

9. Rewrite this name correctly.  ms rosa flores

   _____

10. Use a conjunction to join these sentences. Write the compound sentence.

    Saint Mark's Cathedral is in Venice. The Westminster Abbey is in London.

    _____

    _____

11. Underline two antonyms in the sentence.

    Howard's elegant Tudor looked a little out of place among the plain row houses.

12. Add proper punctuation – a comma, quotation marks, an apostrophe, and an end mark – to complete this sentence.

    Rosa asked Where are all the puppys toys

# Lesson #23

Study the chart; then choose one of the examples to match its definition.

| Root | Meaning | Examples |
|------|---------|----------|
| *post* | after | postbellum, postpone |
| *neo* | new | neophyte, neotype |
| *pre* | before | precooked, pretest |

1. put off until later  _____

2. to test beforehand  _____

3. a "new type" used as a replacement  _____

4. What is the possessive pronoun in this sentence?  _____

    Tia thought she lost her wallet, but it was under the chair you were sitting in.

5. Add commas and quotation marks to this dialogue.

    Reggie asked Where is the closest grocery?

    There's one about a mile from here answered Susie.

6. Is the demonstrative used as a **pronoun** or an **adjective**?

    These lemons are so tart!

    _____

7. What is plagiarism?

   A) using another person's work illegally
   B) online research
   C) a type of report
   D) all of these

8. What is the direct object in this sentence?

   It was raining, so we watched a movie and played indoors.

   A) raining
   B) movie
   C) indoors
   D) There is no direct object in this sentence.

9 – 12. Imagine that you are walking along a beach, and you find a message in a bottle. Brainstorm some ideas for a story about the message in a bottle. Who wrote the message? What part of the world did it come from? When was the message written, and how long has the bottle been floating around? What does the message say? Write your notes in the space below.

_____

_____

_____

_____

_____

_____

_____

_____

_____

# Lesson #24

1. Check the spelling of these words.  If a word is misspelled, cross it out and write it correctly on the line.

    changable        merryment        beautiful

    _____

2. Choose the verb that agrees with the indefinite pronoun.

    One of the trees (was / were) uprooted during the storm.

Choose *linking*, *helping*, or *action* to tell what kind of verb is underlined in each sentence.

3. You may <u>have</u> thought the cheetah was the fastest animal on earth.

    linking        helping        action

4. However, the peregrine falcon <u>is</u> faster.

    linking        helping        action

5. It <u>can</u> dive at a speed of over 200 miles per hour!

    linking        helping        action

6. Cheetahs <u>run</u> faster than any other four-legged animal.

    linking        helping        action

**Summer Solutions© Grammar & Writing** — Level 5

7. How many independent clauses are in this sentence? _____
   Underline each simple subject and verb.

   The sloth is a very slow-moving animal, and the sailfish is a fast-swimming fish.

**Remember, an adverb modifies a verb; a preposition begins a prepositional phrase.**

8. Is the underlined word an *adverb* or a *preposition*?

   It's a beautiful day; go <u>outside</u> for awhile.

   adverb          preposition

9. Is the underlined word an *adverb* or a *preposition*?

   You can play in the yard, but stay <u>inside</u> the gated area.

   adverb          preposition

10. Complete the analogy.

    grape : vine :: peach : _____

    fruit          tree          pit

11. Use what you know about the prefix *pre-* to make the best choice. When would <u>preparatory</u> arrangements be made?

    A) before an event          C) after an event
    B) during an event          D) none of these

12. **Proof It!**

    you did good on your test, and your oral report was interesting

    Is this sentence correct?          Yes          No
    If the sentence has errors, correct them with editing marks.

# Lesson #25

1. Use what you know about the prefix *neo-* to make the best choice. Where would you be likely to find *neologisms*?

   A) a history book
   B) a newly published dictionary
   C) a museum
   D) none of these

2. Add a comma or exclamation mark after each interjection.

   Wow  the beach is packed today!
   Look  There are dolphins out there.

3. Choose the verb that agrees with the indefinite pronoun.

   I have a cold and nothing (taste / tastes) good right now.

4. What does an interrogative do?

   A) tells something
   B) asks something
   C) gives a command
   D) shows strong feeling

5. Underline two antonyms in the sentence.

   The courteous children were shocked by the new boy's impolite behavior.

6. Underline the adverb in this sentence.

   The necklace broke, and the beads rolled everywhere!

7. What does the adverb in the item above tell?

   how    when    where    to what extent

8. Underline the prepositional phrase.

   We could hear the music playing throughout the house.

9. The direct object receives the action of the verb. Underline the direct object.

   Simon caught a frog down near the pond.

10. Add quotation marks and an exclamation mark.

    Abe cried, Stop The glass is overflowing.

These sentences have been edited. Rewrite them correctly.

11. Dolphins swim in the Øcean, but (there) [sp] not fish.

    _____

    _____

12. dolphins are mammals, and ^they seem to like humans.

    _____

    _____

# Lesson #26

1. Use what you know about the prefix *post-* to make the best choice. Which of these is true of a <u>posthumous</u> award?

    A) It is given for humor.
    B) It is given after a person has died.
    C) It always includes money.
    D) none of these

Write these nouns in their proper places in the chart below.

campaign    Election Days    voters    Senator Martin

|   |   | Singular | Plural |
|---|---|----------|--------|
| 2. | Common |  |  |
| 3. | Proper |  |  |

4. Sort these words into two categories.

    muggy    busily    sunny    sandy    perfectly    lazily

    Adverbs    _____

    Adjectives _____

5. Is the demonstrative used as an *adjective* or a *pronoun*?

    I saw that movie last summer.

    adjective        pronoun

6. Write the two past tense forms of the verb *shrink* (*Help Pages*).

    _____, has _____

7. What is the direct object in this sentence?

> If you go shopping, buy some pretzels.

A) shopping

B) some

C) pretzels

D) There is no direct object in this sentence.

8 – 12. A Hydra is a nine-headed monster from Greek Mythology. Imagine that one day you meet a Hydra that can talk. Write a short story about what you and the Hydra might talk about. If dialogue is part of your story, be sure to use quotation marks correctly.

_____

_____

_____

_____

_____

_____

_____

_____

_____

_____

# Lesson #27

1. Combine the sentences with a conjunction, and write a compound sentence below.

    Marcos has collected books all his life.  He has his own library.

    _____

    _____

Study the chart; then choose one of the examples to match its definition.

| Root | Meaning | Examples |
|------|---------|----------|
| vac | empty | vacant, evacuate |
| centi | one hundred | centimeter, century |
| dict | say | diction, dictate |

2. (verb) to empty out completely _____

3. (noun) speech _____

4. (noun) one hundred years _____

5. Add a comma, quotation marks, and an end mark to this sentence.

    Kyle wrote a poem called My Own Shadow

6. Underline two antonyms in the sentence.

    After the race I felt exhausted, but I was invigorated by the cheering of the crowd.

Summer Solutions© Grammar & Writing									Level 5

Look at the underlined words.  Decide whether each word is used as a *noun*, an *adjective*, or a *verb*.  Then write the words in the proper categories.

Even though <u>water</u> is a <u>renewable</u> resource, the amount of <u>clean</u> drinking water is limited, so it is important not to <u>waste</u> water.  You can <u>conserve</u> water by fixing <u>leaky</u> <u>faucets</u> and by shutting off the faucet while you <u>brush</u> your <u>teeth</u>.

7. Nouns _____

8. Adjectives _____

9. Verbs _____

10. Choose the possessive pronoun that agrees with the indefinite subject pronoun.

    Either Kai or Cayden will bring
    (his / their) catcher's mitt and a baseball.

11. Which is correct?

    A)  Amalie could've done better if she had practiced her diving.

    B)  She might'a thought it would be easier than it was.

    C)  Both are correct.

12. Underline the prepositional phrase.  Circle the object of the preposition.

    Take a walk around the house, and count the lights that are turned on.

55

# Lesson #28

1. Use what you know about the root *cent* to make the best choice. What has a *centenarian* done?

   A) written a book
   B) crossed an ocean
   C) lived for 100 years
   D) been elected to government

2. Which is correct?

   A) Their neighbors moved in yesterday.
   B) They neighbors moved in yesterday.
   C) There neighbors moved in yesterday.

3. Write the words that make up the contraction. _____

   It probably <u>would've</u> been easier to travel by train.

4. **Adding the suffix *-ly* to an adjective <u>usually</u> changes the word into an adverb.** Write the adverb formed from these adjectives.

   stupid → _____    playful → _____    light → _____

5. Which of the phrases will make the sentence true?

   In order to avoid plagiarism you should never turn in something that __.

   A) you copied from a book.
   B) you downloaded from the internet.
   C) is not your own work.
   D) All of the phrases would make the sentence true.

6. Cross out the adjective that makes no sense.

   My dog is much (playfuller / more playful) than my cat.

7. Make a list of at least five linking verbs. Look in the Help Pages if you can't think of five.

   _____

8 – 12. **Writing an Invitation**   Write an invitation to a family reunion, birthday party, camp-out, or some other event. Use the format below to make sure you have included all necessary information.

**Who?** (Tell who is invited.) _____

_____

**What?** (Explain the event.) _____

_____

**When?** (Give the starting and ending times.) _____

_____

**Where?** (Tell where the event will take place.) _____

_____

**Why?** (Explain the purpose of the event.) _____

_____

# Lesson #29

1. Find these words in a thesaurus or dictionary. Underline the word that best completes the sentence.

   prismatic    orb    tableau

   The full moon appeared as a perfect, luminous _____ in the night sky.

2. Choose the correct pronoun to complete the sentence.

   One of the girls gave me (their / her) chair.

3. Complete the analogy.

   frog : amphibian :: turtle : _____

   fish    mammal    reptile

4. Underline the adverb; write the verb it modifies.    _____

   The ophthalmologist thoroughly examined my eyes.

5. Match these word parts with their meanings.

   *ped-*      one
   *mono-*     feet
   *trans-*    across

6. Choose the verb that agrees with the subject.

   Gloria made brownies, but she has (hided / hidden / hid) them from us!

7. **The direct object receives the action of the verb.** Underline the direct object.

   Can we climb Mount Rushmore?

8. Use the groups of words below to write a compound sentence.

   we have to be home by 3:00     after our swimming lessons

   we can walk to the Dairy Dream

   _____

   _____

   _____

Look at the following list of nouns and decide how each one fits in the chart below. Write each noun where it belongs in the chart. The first one has been done for you.

Nela Park    memories    Brazilian's    baseball    families'

| | Noun | Common | Proper | Abstract | Possessive | Singular | Plural |
|---|---|---|---|---|---|---|---|
| | Nela Park | | ✓ | | | ✓ | |
| 9. | | ✓ | | ✓ | | | ✓ |
| 10. | | ✓ | | | | ✓ | |
| 11. | | ✓ | | | ✓ | | ✓ |
| 12. | | | ✓ | | ✓ | ✓ | |

# Lesson #30

1. Choose the adverb which completes this sentence.

   You did the assignment (wrong / badly).

2. Choose the superlative that is correct.

   Olivia is much (agreeabler / more agreeable) after her nap.

3. The direct object receives the action of the verb. Underline two direct objects.

   On Friday, the campers pitched their tents; on Saturday, they caught some fish.

4. Why are there two direct objects in the sentence above?

   A) It is a compound sentence.
   B) There are two action verbs.
   C) Both A and B are true.

5. Check the spelling of these words. If a word is misspelled, cross it out and write it correctly on the line.

   commited     traceable     fateful

   _____

6. Which set of words is a prepositional phrase?

   _____ over my shoulder

   _____ turn around

   _____ go outside

Write these nouns in their proper places in the chart below.

Americans   Utah   citizens   taxpayer

|    |        | Singular | Plural |
|----|--------|----------|--------|
| 7. | Common |          |        |
| 8. | Proper |          |        |

9. Look at the underlined word. What part of speech is it?

    Our trip to Disney World was a <u>fabulous</u> vacation!

    _____

Choose *helping*, *action*, or *linking* to tell which kind of verb is underlined in each sentence.

10. Soon school <u>will</u> be starting; I will get to see all my friends.

    helping        action        linking

11. This year will be my best year because I <u>am</u> a great writer!

    helping        action        linking

12. I <u>work</u> hard every day, and I am ready for the sixth grade.

    helping        action        linking

# Summer Solutions.

*Minutes a Day-Mastery for a Lifetime!*

# Level 5

## English Grammar & Writing Mechanics

## Help Pages

# Help Pages

| Parts of Speech | |
|---|---|
| Noun | a word that names a person, place, or thing |
| Verb | a word that shows action or a state of being; a verb is the main word in the predicate of the sentence |
| Pronoun | a word that takes the place of a noun |
| Adjective | a word that describes a noun; an *article* is a special type of adjective (*a, an, the*) |
| Adverb | a word that describes a verb (often ends in *–ly*) (*see* next page) |
| Conjunction | a word that connects words or phrases in a sentence (*and, or, but, so*) |
| Preposition | a word that relates a noun or pronoun to other words in a sentence (*see* list of common prepositions); A *prepositional phrase* begins with a preposition and ends with a noun or pronoun. |
| Interjection | a word or short phrase that shows emotion (*Wow! Aha! Oh no!*) |
| Linking Verb | a word that connects words in a sentence but does not show action; If the verb is a linking verb, there is no direct object. Some verbs that *can be used* as linking verbs are all the forms of *be, appear, become, feel, seem, smell, taste,* and *sound*. |

| Editing Marks | |
|---|---|
| Make capital | ≡ |
| Add end punctuation | ⊙ ! ? |
| Add something | ∧ |
| Make lower case | / |
| Take something out | ⌒ |
| Check spelling | sp |
| Indent | ¶ |

| Helping Verbs | | |
|---|---|---|
| is | can | may |
| are | could | might |
| am | should | have |
| was | would | has |
| were | will | had |
| be | shall | |

# Help Pages

## Adverbs

**Adverbs** tell *how* or *to what extent* and often end in *-ly*. Adverbs can also tell *when* or *where*.

| | |
|---|---|
| How | crazily, merrily, somehow, clumsily, correctly, sadly, quickly, beautifully |
| To What Extent | totally, completely, thoroughly, somewhat |
| When | yesterday, tomorrow, later, often, usually, again, first, next, then |
| Where | here, there, everywhere, somewhere, inside, outside, forward, back |

## Irregular Comparisons

Comparatives and superlatives that do not use *-er* or *-est*:

| | | |
|---|---|---|
| bad | worse | worst |
| good | better | best |
| little | less | least |
| much | more | most |

## Forms of the Verb *Be*

| Present | Past | Future |
|---|---|---|
| am | was | will be |
| is | were | |
| are | | |

## Steps in the Writing Process

| | | |
|---|---|---|
| 1. | Prewriting | getting ideas for writing |
| 2. | Drafting | putting ideas into writing |
| 3. | Revising | adding or taking out words to make the writing better |
| 4. | Editing | using editing marks to correct mistakes |
| 5. | Publishing | sharing the writing with others |

## Verb Tenses

| | |
|---|---|
| Present Tense | Most present tense verbs end in *-s* when the subject is singular. (run - runs) |
| Past Tense | Verbs that tell an action that has already happened usually add *-ed* to show past time. |
| Future Tense | Verbs that tell about an action that is going to happen add the helping verb *will* to show future time. |

# Help Pages

## Spelling Rules

### Rules for Forming Plurals

1. Words ending in *s, x, z, ch,* or *sh,* add *–es* to make the plural.

2. Many words that end in *–f* or *–fe* form the plural by changing the *–f* or *–fe* to *–ves*. **Example**: thief - thieves  Some nouns that end in *–f* or *–ff* do not follow the rule for making plurals. **Examples**: cliff - cliffs, belief - beliefs

3. Some nouns that end in a consonant + *-o* form the plural by adding *–s*. **Example**: zero - zeros; others add *–es*. **Example**: tomato - tomatoes

4. Irregular plural nouns have a completely different spelling in the plural form. **Examples**: ox - oxen, goose - geese, louse - lice

### Other Spelling Rules

5. Place *i* before *e*, except after *c*, or when sounded like *ā* as in *neighbor* and *weigh*. **Examples**: mischief, eight, receive

6. Regular verbs show past tense by adding *–ed*. **Example**: stop - stopped
Irregular verbs change their spelling in the past tense. (*see* **Irregular Verbs**)

7. When adding a prefix to a word, do not change the spelling of the prefix or the root. **Example**:  mis- + step → misstep

8. If a word ends in a vowel + *–y*, add a suffix without changing the spelling of the word. **Example**: employ + -er → employer

9. If a word ends in a consonant + *–y*, change the *y* to *i* before adding suffixes such as *–es, -er,* or *–est*. **Example**: try + *es* → tries
If the suffix begins with an *–i*, do not change the *–y* to *–i*.
**Example**: hurry + *ing* → hurrying

10. There are many exceptions to spelling rules. If you are not sure of the spelling of a word, use a dictionary to check.

## Rules for Using Quotation Marks

1. Put quotation marks before and after the actual words that someone says. Think of quotation marks as the frame around spoken words. Keep the end mark inside the quotes. **Example**: "Don't spoil the fun!"

2. Use the rules for capitalization within quotation marks. Always begin a sentence inside quotation marks with a capital letter.

3. Capitalize proper nouns, the pronoun *I*, and titles, etc. that are inside quotation marks.

# Help Pages

| Rules for Using Quotation Marks (con't) |
| --- |
| 4. If a word is not a proper noun and is not at the beginning of a sentence, do not capitalize. **Example**: "That intersection is dangerous," warned Betsy, "so hold your sister's hand." |
| 5. Use a comma before or after a quote within a sentence. (*see above*) |
| 6. Do not use a comma at the end of the quote if there is another punctuation mark. **Example**: "Grandma's here!" exclaimed Sasha. |

| Rules for Using Commas |
| --- |
| 1. Use commas to separate words or phrases in a series. **Example**: Sun brought a coloring book, some crayons, a pair of scissors, and a ruler. |
| 2. Use a comma to separate two independent clauses joined by a conjunction. **Example**: Dad works in the city, and he is a commuter. |
| 3. Use a comma after an introductory word, such as an interjection. **Example**: Hey, who wants to play tennis? Do not use a comma if there is an end mark after the interjection. **Example**: Oh no! It's starting to rain. |
| 4. Use a comma to separate two words or two numbers, when writing a date. **Example**: Friday, April 8, 2011 |
| 5. Use commas between adjectives if the order doesn't matter. **Example**: the exciting, fresh dance moves (This could also read: fresh, exciting dance moves or exciting *and* fresh dance moves.) |
| 6. Do not use commas between adjectives that describe in different ways. **Example**: three green tomatoes (*Three* tells how many and *green* describes the color.) |
| 7. Insert a comma after introductory words or phrases in a sentence. **Example**: On the other hand, you may not need any help. |
| 8. Use commas before and after "interrupting phrases" within a sentence. **Example**: Ms. Cole, *the bank teller*, was very helpful. |
| 9. Use commas before and/or after contrasting phrases that use *not*. **Example**: I worked on my science project, *not my essay*, all evening. |

# Help Pages

| Pronouns |||
|---|---|---|
| **Type** | Singular | Plural |
| **Subject Pronouns** (or Nominative Case Pronouns) are used as the subject of a sentence or clause. | I, you, he, she, it | we, you, they |
| **Object Pronouns** (or Objective Case Pronouns) are found in the predicate of a sentence. | me, you, him, her, it | us, you, them |
| **Possessive Pronouns** are used to show possession. These possessive pronouns modify a noun. | my, your, his, her, its | our, their, whose |
| **\*\*These possessive pronouns are used alone. | mine, yours, his, hers | ours, theirs, whose |
| **Indefinite Pronouns** replace nouns that are not specific. They can be either singular or plural. ||||
| **Singular**: another, anybody, anyone, anything, each, either, everybody, everyone, everything, little, much, neither, nobody, no one, nothing, one, other, somebody, someone, something ||
| **Plural**: both, few, many, others, several ||
| **Singular or Plural**: all, any, more, most, none, some ||
| **Relative Pronouns** are used to relate a clause to an antecedent. **Example**: the room *which* is next to ours (*which* is the relative pronoun; *room* is the antecedent.) | that, which, who, whom, whose ||
| **Interrogative Pronouns** are used to ask a question. | what, which, who, whom, whose ||
| **Demonstrative Pronouns** are used to point out something. **Example**: *That* is my house. Demonstratives can also be adjectives. **Examples**: *those* flowers, *this* vase | this, that, these, those ||

# Help Pages

| Analogies |
|---|
| An **analogy** is a way of comparing things.<br>Here is an example:    mayor : city :: governor : state<br>You say,<br>    "*Mayor* is to *city* as *governor* is to *state*."<br>To solve an analogy, you need to figure out what the relationship is between the two words.<br>A *mayor* is the leader of a *city*. A *governor* is the leader of a *state*. |
| Here is another example:    lamb : sheep :: calf : _____<br>    horse    piglet    cow    kitten<br>What is the relationship?    A *lamb* is a baby *sheep*.<br>    The missing word must be *cow* because a *calf* is a baby *cow*. |
| In an **analogy**, the words may be compared in many ways.<br>The words may be synonyms.<br>    **Example**:    happy : joyful :: tall : high<br>    *Happy* and *joyful* are synonyms. *Tall* and *high* are synonyms, too. |
| The words may be antonyms.<br>    **Example**:    thin : thick :: rich : poor<br>    *Thin* is the opposite of *thick*. *Rich* is the opposite of *poor*. |
| One word may describe the other.<br>    **Example**:    bright : sunshine :: prickly : porcupine<br>    *Sunshine* is *bright*. A *porcupine* is *prickly*. |
| One word may name a part of the other.<br>    **Example**:    wheels : bicycle :: legs : table<br>    A *bicycle* has *wheels*. A *table* has *legs*. |
| One word may be in the category or group of the other.<br>    **Example**:    rabbit : mammal :: orange : fruit<br>    A *rabbit* is a type of *mammal*. An *orange* is a type of *fruit*. |

# Help Pages

| | |
|---|---|
| **Plagiarism** | **Plagiarism** is the illegal use of another person's words, putting your name on someone else's work, copying another person's words or work, or not giving credit to a source. |
| **Abbreviations** | An **abbreviation** is a shortened form of a word. Some abbreviations, such as social titles, months, and weekdays, end in a period.<br><br>**Examples**: Dr., Mr., Ms., and Mrs. / Sept., Mon., Feb. Thurs. Postal abbreviations do not end in a period. AK, OH, PA, WV |

### Figures of Speech

| | |
|---|---|
| **Simile** | A **simile** is a way to describe something by using a comparison. A simile compares two things using the words *like* or *as*.<br>**Example**: The baby is *as playful as a kitten*.<br>(The baby is being compared to a kitten.) |
| **Idiom** | An **idiom** has a special meaning in a certain language. It is not a literal meaning. For example, in the United States we say, "Now you will have to *face the music*." This statement has nothing to do with music. It means someone has to deal with the consequences of his/her actions. |
| **Metaphor** | A **metaphor** compares two things but does not use *like* or *as*. It uses a form of the verb *be*.<br>**Example**: Joey is a magnet for bad luck.<br>(Joey attracts bad luck.) |
| **Hyperbole** | **Hyperbole** uses exaggeration to make a point.<br>**Example**: My book bag weighs a ton! |

### Common Prepositions

| | | | | | |
|---|---|---|---|---|---|
| about | before | down | near | past | up |
| above | behind | during | of | through | upon |
| across | below | except | off | throughout | with |
| after | beneath | for | on | to | within |
| against | beside | from | onto | toward | without |
| along | between | in | out | under | |
| among | beyond | inside | outside | underneath | |
| around | by | into | over | until | |

# Help Pages

| Irregular Verbs ||| 
| :---: | :---: | :---: |
| **Present** | **Past** | **With *has*, *have*, or *had*** |
| awake | awoke | *has, have,* or *had* awoken |
| become | became | *has, have,* or *had* become |
| build | built | *has, have,* or *had* built |
| catch | caught | *has, have,* or *had* caught |
| creep | crept | *has, have,* or *had* crept |
| drink | drank | *has, have,* or *had* drunk |
| fall | fell | *has, have,* or *had* fallen |
| fight | fought | *has, have,* or *had* fought |
| forbid | forbade | *has, have,* or *had* forbidden |
| get | got | *has, have,* or *had* gotten |
| hide | hid | *has, have,* or *had* hidden |
| keep | kept | *has, have,* or *had* kept |
| leave | left | *has, have,* or *had* left |
| mistake | mistook | *has, have,* or *had* mistaken |
| ride | rode | *has, have,* or *had* ridden |
| shake | shook | *has, have,* or *had* shaken |
| shrink | shrank | *has, have,* or *had* shrunk |
| sneak | sneaked (snuck) | *has, have,* or *had* sneaked (snuck) |
| stink | stank | *has, have,* or *had* stunk |
| sweep | swept | *has, have,* or *had* swept |
| teach | taught | *has, have,* or *had* taught |
| understand | understood | *has, have,* or *had* understood |
| wind | wound | *has, have,* or *had* wound |

# Summer Solutions

## Level 5

### English Grammar & Writing Mechanics

### Answers to Lessons

# Summer Solutions© Grammar & Writing — Level 5

| | Lesson #1 | | Lesson #2 | | Lesson #3 |
|---|---|---|---|---|---|
| 1 | ✓ Gaunt rhymes with haunt.<br>✓ The opposite of gaunt is plump. | 1 | <u>clear</u> | 1 | <u>amplify</u> |
| 2 | My mother, wherever she is, will expect a phone… | 2 | Michael, our skateboard instructor, won't… | 2 | Troy Smith, the Heisman Trophy winner,… |
| 3 | <u>were</u> | 3 | have | 3 | (university) |
| 4 | should have | 4 | could've | 4 | it's   she'll   they'd |
| 5 | B | 5 | shortly<br>wildly<br>pleasantly | 5 | <u>The House of Representatives</u> |
| 6 | D | 6 | (well)   new | 6 | adjective |
| 7 | linking | 7 | Richard is great at building things, and (so) he wants to be an architect. | 7 | more upset |
| 8 | action | 8 | (Larry) | 8 | June 11 |
| 9 | helping | 9 | <u>He survived in the wilderness for several weeks.</u> | 9 | Yes. June 11, 12, 26, 27, 28 |
| 10 | adverb | 10 | ~~No camping gear, food, or cell phone.~~ | 10 | June 10, 16, 17 23, 24, 30 |
| 11 | Krissy is going to join "Vacation Bookworms." | 11 | He had no camping gear, food, or cell phone. (Answers may vary.) | 11 | Saturday,  Sunday |
| 12 | It's a book club that meets at the library all summer. | 12 | i̲   (run)^sp | 12 | B |

74

# Summer Solutions© Grammar & Writing — Level 5

| | Lesson #4 | | Lesson #5 | | Lesson #6 |
|---|---|---|---|---|---|
| 1 | mischief | 1 | colder | 1 | C |
| 2 | What   where | 2 | …rolls, my mother's favorite,… | 2 | C |
| 3 | ~~shoulda'~~   ~~would'nt~~ | 3 | worse | 3 | E |
| 4 | grow nicely near the tree line. | 4 | They | 4 | C |
| 5 | carefully   Read | 5 | I've | 5 | A |
| 6 | better | 6 | arrived | 6 | they had   he will |
| 7 | D | 7 | A | 7 | ✓ The h in archaic is silent.<br>✓ Archaic means "out-of-date." |
| 8 | Oh no! | 8 | C | 8 | B |
| 9 | B | 9 | A | 9 | patiently   wait |
| 10 | Having Theresa around … an extra set of hands | 10 | B | 10 | best |
| 11 | ✓ Yes   tree house | 11 | C | 11 | ~~The leader of the free world.~~ |
| 12 | A tree house is a great place to read a book or (and) to take a nap. | 12 | A | 12 | a predicate |

| | Lesson #7 | | Lesson #8 | | Lesson #9 |
|---|---|---|---|---|---|
| 1 | ...fruit, not vegetables, at ... | 1 | Maureen, not Aunt Chloe, will... | 1 | A) A<br>B) P |
| 2 | (friend) (companion) | 2 | solemn | 2 | fact |
| 3 | that  phone number | 3 | understood<br>understood | 3 | , but |
| 4 | we'd<br>you'd<br>they'd | 4 | Our spring concert/ featured... | 4 | dr.  saturdays |
| 5 | A | 5 | adjective - funny<br>adverb - foolishly | 5 | (Braces) |
| 6 | Theresa   lifesaver | 6 | dreams | 6 | DE   Delaware<br>PR   Puerto Rico<br>AL   Alabama |
| 7 | A | 7 | bicycle | 7 | verb |
| 8 | winter, trails, house | 8 | chipmunks' | 8 | C |
| 9 | funny, snowy | 9 | Asia's | 9 | 8 ingredients (9 including cooking spray) |
| 10 | read, hike | 10 | easiest   craziest | 10 | stir |
| 11 | (noticable) sp<br>(improvments) sp | 11 | -phone - sound<br>-gram - writing<br>-phobia -fear | 11 | cool it completely |
| 12 | Some noticeable improvements were made in the cafeteria. | 12 | Luna is going to get braces as soon as school starts. | 12 | D |

# Summer Solutions© Grammar & Writing — Level 5

| | Lesson #10 | | Lesson #11 | | Lesson #12 |
|---|---|---|---|---|---|
| 1 | Europe | 1 | effect | 1 | B) postpone<br>C) polymorphic<br>A) phobic |
| 2 | have not   did not | 2 | …napkins, not paper,… | 2 | Whom |
| 3 | Declarative<br>Imperative<br>Exclamatory<br>Interrogative | 3 | that   key | 3 | were not   was not |
| 4 | throughout the (Midwest) | 4 | won't   doesn't | 4 | B |
| 5 | A) adjective<br>B) adverb | 5 | The senators from Ohio | 5 | when |
| 6 | D | 6 | You | 6 | irish |
| 7 | a   an   the | 7 | gal.<br>yd. | 7 | but |
| 8 | the tree's roots<br>the puppy's toys | 8 | tsp. (t.)<br>oz. | 8 | B |
| 9 | got   gotten | 9 | doz.<br>Tbsp. (T.) | 9 | …clothesline, not… |
| 10 | -port → not<br>geo- ✕ carry<br>non- → earth | 10 | shaken | 10 | Has |
| 11 | tricks | 11 | pronoun | 11 | isn't<br>aren't |
| 12 | Peggi really enjoyed playing golf and hanging out with her friends. | 12 | wolves   roofs | 12 | played   (game) |

# Summer Solutions© Grammar & Writing — Level 5

| | Lesson #13 | | Lesson #14 | | Lesson #15 |
|---|---|---|---|---|---|
| 1 | outdated | 1 | their | 1 | A) nation<br>B) Navaho |
| 2 | Use sugar, not artificial sweetener,... | 2 | haven't | 2 | C) people<br>D) Indians |
| 3 | C | 3 | nutrition | 3 | <u>sun</u>   <u>grapefruit</u> |
| 4 | old | 4 | The rain fell <u>lightly</u>... there was a <u>light</u>... | 4 | synonyms |
| 5 | No | 5 | <u>joy</u>   <u>memories</u><br><u>pride</u>   <u>generosity</u> | 5 | A) ✓<br>C) ✓ |
| 6 | Adj.   lazy, hopeful, perfect<br>Adv.   merrily, nicely, shortly | 6 | The police car's siren scared the bully away. | 6 | The scarecrow asked, "Have you seen the Wizard?" |
| 7 | "I never get a chance to be the leader," chirped Betsy. | 7 | so | 7 | <u>paint</u>   (deck) |
| 8 | ... really well.<br>...good job of... | 8 | <u>knowledge</u><br><u>proficiency</u><br><u>expertise</u> | 8 - 12 | Answers will vary. |
| 9 | either / or | 9 | and, or, but, so<br>(Any three.) | | |
| 10 | (gratful) sp | 10 | 90 calories | | |
| 11 - 12 | <u>I wish that I could get a robot that would do three things every day: clean my room, check my homework, and pack my lunch.</u><br>(Answers will vary.) | 11 | carbohydrates | | |
| | | 12 | B | | |

| Lesson #16 | | Lesson #17 | | Lesson #18 | |
|---|---|---|---|---|---|
| 1 | pedestrian | 1 | Lexie answered, "I got my nickname from my little brother." | 1 | grain |
| 2 | transplant | 2 | antonyms | 2 | unsafe |
| 3 | terra cotta | 3 | C | 3 | They |
| 4 | their | 4 | many, everyone, someone | 4 | Florida is a peninsula, and its name means "full of flowers." |
| 5 | The Mothers Against Drunk Driving | 5 | who, that, which | 5 | Mark's brother, his father, and his grandfather are all firefighters. |
| 6 | for some paper four boxes | 6 | your, their, my | 6 | the |
| 7 | tenderly  lifted | 7 | ~~Shelter, water, food, or safety?~~ | 7 | A |
| 8 | Joyce & Edmond | 8 | thoroughly examined | 8 | ✓ the author's name <br> ✓ the title of the book |
| 9 | Rénee Baer Rita Ferris | 9 | a pomegranate an apricot | 9 | A) cause <br> B) effect |
| 10 | Larry Ferris | 10 | A) C <br> B) E | 10-12 | Answers will vary. |
| 11 | Jeff & Elaine Link | 11 | Columbus was born in Italy, but he sailed from Spain. | | |
| 12 | Rita (Sells) Ferris | 12 | There were three ships: the Nina, the Pinta, and the Santa Maria. | | |

| | Lesson #19 | | Lesson #20 | | Lesson #21 |
|---|---|---|---|---|---|
| 1 | Julia's tortilla soup was made with carrots, onions, peppers, and beans. | 1 - 5 | Answers will vary. | 1 | "Let's walk to the skateboard park," suggested Erica, "and we can get an ice cream cone on the way." |
| 2 | You shouldn't ride your bike without a helmet. | | | 2 | C |
| 3 | Who | | | 3 | It'll |
| 4 | asparagus pencils | | | 4 | well |
| 5 | ~~collecttable~~ ~~hankercheif~~ collectible handkerchief | | | 5 | tidy   campsite |
| 6 | mistaken | 6 | hideous | 6 | It is okay to use information from the internet, but you must use your own words and cite your source. (Answers will vary.) |
| 7 | adverb – pleasantly adjective – lovely | 7 | was | 7 | B |
| 8 | A) fact B) opinion | 8 | children's | 8 | December 21, 2006 |
| 9 | Pete, Mr. Muller, Dr. Lilly | 9 | was | 9 | helping    main    are    hosting |
| 10 | Honolulu, Spain, Pittsburgh | 10 | effect | 10 | (jacket)   that |
| 11 | flash drives, helmet, ivy | 11 | A. linking B. helping C. action | 11 | D |
| 12 | imagination, loyalty, love | 12 | (No) The newest state in the U.S. is Hawaii. | 12 | (No) Josie and I share the same birthday. |

# Summer Solutions© Grammar & Writing — Level 5

| | Lesson #22 | | Lesson #23 | | Lesson #24 |
|---|---|---|---|---|---|
| 1 | A) adverb  B) preposition | 1 | postpone | 1 | ~~changable~~ ~~merryment~~  changeable  merriment |
| 2 | linking | 2 | pretest | 2 | was |
| 3 | action | 3 | neotype | 3 | helping |
| 4 | helping | 4 | her | 4 | linking |
| 5 | The Bank of China in Hong Kong | 5 | Reggie asked, "Where...grocery?" "There's...here," answered Susie. | 5 | helping |
| 6 | justly | 6 | adjective | 6 | action |
| 7 | (Chrysler Building)  gigantic | 7 | A | 7 | 2  sloth  is  sailfish  is |
| 8 | The world's tallest building is in Taiwan. | 8 | B | 8 | adverb |
| 9 | Ms. Rosa Flores | 9-12 | Answers will vary. | 9 | preposition |
| 10 | Saint Mark's Cathedral is in Venice, but (and) the Westminster Abbey is in London. | | | 10 | tree |
| 11 | elegant  plain | | | 11 | A |
| 12 | Rosa asked, "Where are all the puppy's toys?" | | | 12 | (No) you did ~~good~~ well on your test, and your oral report was interesting⊙ |

81

| | Lesson #25 | | Lesson #26 | | Lesson #27 |
|---|---|---|---|---|---|
| 1 | B | 1 | B | 1 | Marcos has collected books all his life, and (so) he has his own library. |
| 2 | Wow, the… Look! There… | 2 | s → campaign<br>pl → voters | 2 | evacuate |
| 3 | tastes | 3 | s → Senator Martin<br>pl → Election Days | 3 | diction |
| 4 | B | 4 | Adv. → busily, lazily, perfectly<br>Adj. → muggy, sunny, sandy | 4 | century |
| 5 | courteous   impolite | 5 | adjective | 5 | Kyle wrote a poem called, "My Own Shadow." |
| 6 | everywhere | 6 | shrank,  shrunk | 6 | exhausted invigorated |
| 7 | where | 7 | C | 7 | water, faucets, teeth |
| 8 | throughout the house | 8-12 | Answers will vary. | 8 | renewable, clean, leaky |
| 9 | frog | | | 9 | waste, conserve, brush |
| 10 | Abe cried, "Stop! The glass is overflowing." | | | 10 | his |
| 11 | Dolphins swim in the ocean, but they're not fish. | | | 11 | A |
| 12 | Dolphins are mammals, and they seem to like humans. | | | 12 | around the (house) |

| | Lesson #28 | | Lesson #29 | | Lesson #30 |
|---|---|---|---|---|---|
| 1 | C | 1 | <u>orb</u> | 1 | badly |
| 2 | A | 2 | her | 2 | more agreeable |
| 3 | would have | 3 | reptile | 3 | <u>tents</u>   <u>fish</u> |
| 4 | stupidly<br>playfully<br>lightly | 4 | <u>thoroughly</u> examined | 4 | C |
| 5 | D | 5 | ped — one<br>mono ✗ feet<br>trans — across | 5 | ~~committed~~<br>committed |
| 6 | ~~playfuller~~ | 6 | hidden | 6 | ✓ over my shoulder |
| 7 | taste, smell, feel, become, is, was, etc.<br>(List of five will vary.) | 7 | <u>Mount Rushmore</u> | 7 | taxpayer   citizens |
| 8 - 12 | (Any five.) | 8 | Answers will vary. | 8 | Utah   Americans |
| | | 9 | memories | 9 | adjective |
| | | 10 | baseball | 10 | helping |
| | | 11 | families' | 11 | linking |
| | | 12 | Brazilian's | 12 | action |